M000018117

Forever Grateful To You: